DOCUMENTING
U.S. HISTORY

THE **MAYFLOWER COMPACT**

Elizabeth Raum

Heinemann
LIBRARY

Chicago, Illinois

www.capstonepub.com
Visit our website to find out more information about Heinemann-Raintree books.

To order:
☎ Phone 800-747-4992
💻 Visit www.capstonepub.com to browse our catalog and order online.

Edited by Abby Colich, Megan Cotugno, and Laura Hensley
Designed by Cynthia Della-Rovere
Original illustrations © Capstone Global Library
    Limited 2011
Illustrated by Oxford Designers & Illustrators
Picture research by Tracy Cummins
Originated by Capstone Global Library Limited
Printed and bound in China by CTPS

16 15 14 13 12
10 9 8 7 6 5 4 3 2 1

Library of Congress Cataloging-in-Publication Data
Raum, Elizabeth.
   The Mayflower Compact / Elizabeth Raum.
      p. cm.—(Documenting U.S. history)
   Includes bibliographical references and index.
   ISBN 978-1-4329-6750-5 (hb)—ISBN 978-1-4329-6759-8 (pb) 1. Mayflower Compact (1620)—Juvenile literature. 2. Pilgrims (New Plymouth Colony)—Juvenile literature. 3. Mayflower (Ship)—Juvenile literature. 4. Massachusetts—History—New Plymouth, 1620-1691—Juvenile literature. I. Title.
   F68.R38 2012
   974.4'8202—dc23   2011037778

Acknowledgments
The author and publishers are grateful to the following for permission to reproduce copyright material: Alamy: pp. 14 (© North Wind Picture Archives), 23 right (© STUART WALKER), 32 (© North Wind Picture Archives); Corbis: pp. 4 (© Bettmann), 6 (© Bettmann), 8 (© Alfredo Dagli Orti/ The Art Archive), 15 (© Corbis), 19 (© Bettmann), 29 (© Lee Snider/Photo Images); Courtesy of the State Library of Massachusetts: p. 21; Getty Images: pp. 12 (Universal History Archive), 17 (The Bridgeman Art Library), 23 left (Three Lions), 27 (Archive Photos), 36 (MPI), 41 (Ralph Orlowski); istockphoto: p. 37 (© Stephen Orsillo); Library of Congress Prints and Photographs Division: p. 30; Pilgrim Hall Museum: pp. 7, 24; Shutterstock: pp. 35 (© Suchan), 39 (© Aeypix), 43 bottom (© Suchan), 43 top (© Suchan); The Granger Collection: pp. 11 bottom, 11 top, 13, 20.

Cover image of passengers of the Mayflower signing the "Mayflower Compact" including Carver, Winston, Alden, Myles Standish, Howland, Bradford, Allerton, and Fuller created by Jean Leon Gerome Ferris reproduced with permission from Library of Congress Prints and Photographs Division. Cover image of the Mayflower Compact reproduced courtesy of the State Library of Massachusetts.

Every effort has been made to contact copyright holders of material reproduced in this book. Any omissions will be rectified in subsequent printings if notice is given to the publisher.

Contents

Some words are printed in **bold**, like this. You can find out what they mean by looking in the glossary.

Recording Important Events

Today, when something important happens, television cameras roll and the event is captured on film. News stories reach people around the world in a matter of minutes. In 1620, when a ship called the *Mayflower* and its passengers landed at Plymouth, in present-day Massachusetts, there were no cameras or reporters to greet them.

This painting shows an artist's idea of how the Mayflower *looked when it sailed to North America in 1620.*

Pilgrim accounts

The **Pilgrims** found their own ways to record important events. They wrote letters, diaries, and journals. In 1622 several Pilgrim men published a small book that included letters and journal entries about their lives in Plymouth. It had a very long title: *A Relation or Journall of the beginning and proceedings of the English Plantation Setled at Plimouth in New England*. This book provides a first-hand account of the Pilgrims' arrival and early life in Plymouth. Edward Winslow, a Pilgrim, probably wrote most of the book and had it printed in England.

Winslow's book includes a copy of the Mayflower **Compact**, one of the earliest documents in U.S. history. By signing the Mayflower Compact, the passengers agreed to work together as a community. The Compact also set up a form of government for the new **colony**.

Know It!

In 1796 a historian renamed Winslow's book. He gave it a shorter name: *Mourt's Relation: A Journal of the Pilgrims at Plymouth*. This title is used today.

Primary sources

Historians use **primary sources** to study the past. Primary sources include official documents, diaries, journals, letters, speeches, photographs, maps, and drawings.

The Mayflower Compact is a primary source document. Winslow's book, now called *Mourt's Relation*, is also a primary source. So is a book called *Of Plymouth Plantation*, written by Plymouth governor William Bradford. The authors were eyewitnesses to history. John Smith's map (below) is also a primary source.

The Pilgrims studied Captain John Smith's map of New England before setting sail on the Mayflower.

This sword belonged to Mayflower passenger John Carver.

Artifacts such as guns, ships, furniture, and clothing are also primary sources. For example, when historians study an artifact such as John Carver's sword (see the photo), they gain a better understanding of how the Pilgrims protected themselves. Understanding small details of everyday life helps historians form a clearer picture of what happened.

Secondary sources

Historians use primary sources to write encyclopedia articles, textbooks, and nonfiction books about the past. These new works are called **secondary sources**. Secondary sources provide important information about particular people, places, and events.

Historians study primary sources so that they can explain history. Artists use primary sources to draw pictures of people, events, and items from the past. Primary source documents provide a direct look into the past. Secondary sources help explain the past.

First Journey: Holland

The Mayflower **Compact** was written by the **colonists** who settled at Plymouth, Massachusetts, in 1620. We call these people **Pilgrims**, but that term was not widely used until about the 1800s.

The Pilgrims

The Pilgrims were made up of two different groups of people from England. The people who organized the trip to North America were **Separatists**. Separatists were **Christians** who believed that people should form **congregations** and organize simple worship services. They did not belong to the official government church, the **Church of England**.

King James I (1567–1625)

At the age of one, James became king of Scotland. His mother, Mary, Queen of Scots, left Scotland the next year and never saw her son again. Scottish advisers helped the child king rule. In 1603, when England's Queen Elizabeth I died, James became king of England. He ruled England and Scotland until his death in 1625.

1603
James I becomes king of England.

1607
Scrooby Separatists are arrested trying to leave England.

1611
The King James Bible is published.

In 1604 King James selected a committee to produce a new Bible (book of sacred Christian writings) in English. This new Bible, called the King James Bible, was completed in 1611. More than 2.6 billion copies have been published. Even though there are many newer English Bibles, the King James Bible is still used today.

England's King James I disagreed. He ordered Separatists to attend the Church of England and to obey church laws. When they refused, James jailed Separatist leaders. The Separatist congregation at Scrooby, England (see the map), left for Holland, rather than obey the king.

This map shows where Pilgrims lived before leaving on the Mayflower *and landing in Plymouth, Massachusetts*

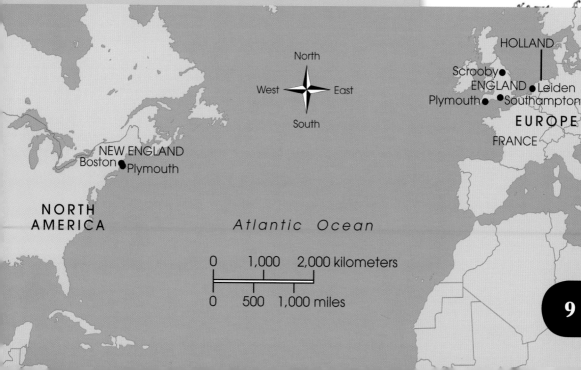

Flight to Holland

The Separatist congregation walked 60 miles (97 kilometers) from Scrooby to a waiting ship on the English coast. Before they boarded the ship, King James's soldiers swooped in, arrested them, and tossed them in jail. The ship's captain had turned them in.

In the spring of 1608, they made another attempt to leave. It wasn't easy. But by the summer, the entire group had reached Holland (see map on page 9).

Life in Leiden

The **Dutch** welcomed the Scrooby congregation. They allowed them to worship as they wanted. In 1609 the congregation moved to Leiden (see map on page 9), a city of about 80,000 people. They found work as button makers, tailors, hatmakers, shoemakers, carpenters, and doing other similar jobs. William Bradford, who later became governor of Plymouth **Colony**, worked as a **weaver**. William Brewster, another Pilgrim leader, ran a printing business. They all worked long hours for very little money.

Know It!

The Separatists often chose names with special meaning. Some of the children who went to North America on the *Mayflower* were named Remember, Patience, Fear (girls), and Love (boys).

William Brewster
(1566–1644)

William Brewster was born in Scrooby. He attended Cambridge University. In 1590 he became Scrooby's postmaster. He was a Separatist who allowed the Scrooby congregation to worship in his home. In North America, he would become the group's religious leader. He often led worship and helped the congregation make important decisions. He died in Plymouth in 1644.

A storm caused rough seas, making the escape to Holland dangerous.

Spring 1608
Separatists begin to successfully leave for Holland.

1609
The Scrooby congregation settles in Leiden.

Deciding to leave

In 1617 the Separatist congregation in Leiden decided to go to North America to seek a better life. They worried that their children were becoming too Dutch. In North America, they could speak English, follow English customs, and practice their own religion.

"So they left that goodly and pleasant city which had been their resting place near twelve years; but they knew they were Pilgrims."

—*William Bradford,* Of Plymouth Plantation. *This passage includes the first use of the word* Pilgrim *to refer to the Plymouth colonists.*

This 1614 drawing shows an area near Leiden University, where the Separatists lived.

1617
The Pilgrims decide to go to North America.

The Virginia Company (see box on right) agreed to loan the Separatists money to pay for travel costs and supplies. The congregation's leaders—William Brewster, William Bradford, and Edward Winslow (see box below)—agreed to repay the company in furs, fish, lumber, and other goods. They agreed to wait seven years to claim land of their own.

Know It!

The Virginia Company was founded by King James I, to help establish North American colonies. In 1607 the Virginia Company founded the colony of Jamestown, Virginia.

Edward Winslow
(1595–1655)

Edward Winslow joined the Separatist congregation in Leiden in 1617. He worked in William Brewster's printing business. He later became a trusted leader among the North American colonists and the native Wampanoag people. Winslow, who wrote much of *Mourt's Relation*, often traveled to England on colony business. He died at sea at age 60.

Second Journey: North America

Only 41 of the Leiden church members agreed to go to North America. Half were children. Other **congregation** members were too old, too ill, or too fearful. In July 1620, 41 **Pilgrims** took a ship called the *Speedwell* from Holland to Southampton, England (see map on page 9). This is where they would meet another ship, the *Mayflower*, and begin the journey to North America.

The strangers

However, 41 people were not enough to begin a **colony**. In London, some relatives joined the original group. The Virginia Company intended to make money from the colony. To do that, it needed workers. The company began **recruiting** anyone who was willing to work, no matter their religious beliefs.

The Pilgrims left Holland on the Speedwell *in July 1620.*

Myles Standish (1584–1656)

The Pilgrims hired Myles Standish, a soldier living in Holland, to be their military leader. He was not a **Separatist**, but he became their loyal supporter. He went on to help explore the New England coast, make peaceful contacts with American Indians, and help protect the colony from attack. He earned the respect of the entire colony. Standish died in Duxbury, in present-day Massachusetts, in 1656.

These additional passengers did not share the religious beliefs of the Leiden congregation. Most of them belonged to the **Church of England**. Many were related to the men in the Virginia Company. They hoped to start a new life in North America. Others were looking for new land and opportunities. A few were servants.

1620
The Pilgrims leave Leiden for a brief stop in England. More passengers join them there.

Leaky ship

On August 15, 1620, the Pilgrims left England on two ships: the *Speedwell* and the *Mayflower*. When the *Speedwell* began to leak, the ships returned to port. After a month of delays, some travelers became so discouraged that they stayed in England. So did the leaky *Speedwell*. On September 16, 1620, the *Mayflower* left England with 102 passengers on board.

Who's in charge?

Christopher Jones, the *Mayflower's* captain, commanded a crew of 20 to 30 seamen. At sea, he was in charge. In the new colony, however, Separatists William Brewster, John Carver, William Bradford, and Edward Winslow would become trusted leaders.

Know It!

Mayflower passengers ate salted meat, dried fish, cheese, and beer. Instead of bread, they ate hardtack, a rock-hard cracker made of flour and water.

"...they were encountered many times with cross winds and met with many fierce storms."

—*William Bradford,* Of Plymouth Plantation

August 15, 1620
The Pilgrims leave England on two ships: the *Speedwell* and the *Mayflower*. The leaky *Speedwell* soon turns back.

The Pilgrims crowded onto the sturdy Mayflower for the trip to North America.

The voyage

At first, many of the passengers suffered from seasickness. They soon recovered, and the first half of the voyage went smoothly. About halfway to North America, bad storms damaged the ship. It developed leaks, and a large beam cracked. Master Jones had the crew make repairs, and the ship sailed on.

The passengers were cold and damp in their crowded quarters below deck. Several passengers became ill. Only one passenger died during the voyage. He was a boy who worked as a servant to the doctor.

Know It!

Of the 102 passengers who sailed to North America, only 69 were adults. There were 14 young people between the ages of 13 and 18, as well as 19 younger children.

September 16, 1620
The *Mayflower* leaves for North America, carrying all the remaining passengers.

The "Combination"

After two months at sea, the crew spotted land. They had reached Cape Cod, in present-day Massachusetts. The **Pilgrims** had a **patent**, or **charter**, to land in the northern part of the Virginia **Colony**. This area did not include Cape Cod. However, bad weather and rough seas convinced them to stay. With or without a charter, this is where they would begin their new life.

Know It!

The term *combination* means a "knitting together" of two groups. A compact was an agreement or understanding between groups of people. Both terms—*combination* and *compact*—had similar meanings in **colonial** days.

Combine together

Some of the people **recruited** by the Virginia Company protested the decision to stay in Cape Cod. Without a patent, they felt free to ignore previous agreements and to go off on their own. Wiser men knew that everyone would be needed to build the colony.

November 9, 1620
The *Mayflower* crew spots land.

This painting shows Mayflower passengers aboard the ship signing the combination.

So before they left the *Mayflower*, William Brewster, a member of the Leiden **congregation**, and Stephen Hopkins, who was not a member, wrote the document now called the Mayflower **Compact**. The passengers called it the "**combination**" because it combined the two groups into a community. It also gave the colony the right to form its own government, make laws, and elect officials. Immediately after signing the Compact, the **colonists** elected John Carver, a **Separatist**, governor of the new colony.

"…it was thought good there should be an association and agreement that we should combine together in one body…"

—Mourt's Relation

November 11, 1620
The *Mayflower* reaches Cape Cod. The Mayflower Compact is drafted and signed by passengers. John Carver is elected governor of Plymouth.

Making it legal

British kings used charters and patents to grant specific rights or privileges. The Pilgrims needed a new patent from England granting rights in the area where they had landed. Until this patent arrived, the Mayflower Compact served as a legal agreement among the Plymouth colonists.

The first European child born in Massachusetts, Peregrine White, slept in a cradle brought from Holland on the Mayflower.

Taking a closer look

But just what did the Compact say? The Compact opens with the words: "In the name of God, Amen." As a religious people, the signers wanted to honor God. They considered God the witness to their agreement.

Know It!

The first baby born to the Plymouth colonists was Peregrine White, son of Susanna and William White. His name, Peregrine, means "traveler" or "pilgrim." The only child born during the ocean voyage was a baby boy named Oceanus Hopkins. *Oceanus* is the Latin word for "ocean."

Next, the document proclaims the people's loyalty to the English king. Even though they had chosen to leave their native land, they intended to remain English and do business as an English colony.

The Mayflower Compact was written almost 400 years ago. Grammar and spelling have changed over the years, but the message is still clear.

Know It!

By June 1621, the Virginia Company provided a new patent granting the Pilgrims rights to Plymouth and the surrounding land. The Mayflower Compact, which was so important in the first days, was no longer needed.

The Mayflower Compact
THE FIRST DECLARATION OF THE PRINCIPLES OF AMERICAN FREEDOM

In y name of god Amen. We whose names are underwritten the loyall subiects of our dread soueraigne Lord King Iames by y grace of god, of great Britaine, franc, & Yreland King defender of y faith, &c

Haueing undertaken, for y glorie of god, and aduancemente of y christian faith and honour of our king & countrie, a voyage to plant y first colonie in y Northerne parts of Virginia. Doe by these presents solemnly & mutualy in y presence of god, and one of another, Couenant & combine our selues togeather into a ciuill body politick; for y better ordering, & preseruation & furtherance of y ends aforsaid; and by vertue hearof to enacte, constitute, and frame shuch just & equall Lawes, ordinances, Acts, constitutions, & offices, from time to time, as shall be thought most meete & convenient for y generall good of y Colonie: unto which we promise all due submission and obedience. In witnes wherof we haue hereunder subscribed our names at cap= Codd y 11 of Nouember, in y year of y raigne of our soueraigne Lord king Iames of England, franc, & Yreland y eighteenth and of scotland y fiftie fourth Ao. dom. 1620.

John Caruer	Richard Warren	Francis Eaton	Richard Britterige
William Bradford	John Howland	James Chilton	Georg Sowle
Edward Winslow	Steuen Hopkins	John Craxton	Richard Clarke
William Brewster	Edward Tillie	John Billinton	Richard Gardenar
Isaack Allerton	John Tillie	Moyses Fletcher	John Allerton
Myles Standish	Francis Cooke	John Goodman	Thomas Enlish
John Alden	Thomas Rogers	Digorie preist	Edward Doty
Samuell Fuller	Thomas Tinker	Thomas Williams	Edward Lister
Christpher Martin	John Ridgale	Gilbart Winslow	
William Mullines	Edward Fuller	Edmond Margeson	
William White	John Turner	Peter Browne	

A pledge to God and one another

In the Mayflower Compact, the Pilgrims pledged to:

- work together as a community

- create laws and elect officials

- hold public meetings for the good of the colony.

They pledged to form a government and to create laws that were good for the community. They called this a "civil body politic." They knew that English laws might not work in North America. Public meetings provided an opportunity for the community to come together to discuss important events. The Pilgrims used these powers immediately by electing John Carver as governor.

"…solemnly and mutually in the presence of God and one of another, covenant [agree], and combine ourselves together into a civil body politic for our better ordering and preservation…"

—Mourt's Relation

November 21, 1620
The Pilgrims sign the Mayflower Compact.

The signatures

The last section of the Compact includes the date and signatures. The first 12 signers ranked highest in terms of wealth and responsibility. These included both Separatists such as Carver, Bradford, and Winslow, as well as non-Separatists such as Standish, Martin, and Hopkins. Next came 27 farmers or laborers. Finally, a few of the servants signed. Women did not sign legal documents at the time.

William Bradford
(1590–1657)

William Bradford, who wrote *Of Plymouth Plantation*, joined the Separatists at age 12 or 13. He went to Holland in 1607 and to North America in 1620. At age 31, he became governor of Plymouth Colony. His wise decisions helped the colony succeed. He died at age 67 in Massachusetts.

These are some of the signatures on the Mayflower Compact.

Plymouth Colony

On the same day that the passengers signed the Mayflower **Compact**, Myles Standish led 16 men ashore. They spent 27 days exploring. They found fresh water, cleared land, and baskets containing Indian corn and beans. They took the corn and beans to use for seeds the following spring. They saw few American Indians.

The **Pilgrims** decided to settle near Plymouth Bay, in present-day Massachusetts. They named their **colony** New Plymouth or Plymouth Plantation. The men began building storehouses and simple huts. Most women and children continued to live on the ship.

Know It!

Beaver hats were worn by both men and women in Europe. The Pilgrims sent beaver furs to England to be made into felt for hats.

Constance Hopkins, who was 13 or 14 when she traveled on the Mayflower, *owned this beaver hat.*

Terrible winter

From 1550 to the 1700s, Massachusetts experienced the Little Ice Age, a period of colder-than-average temperatures. Extreme cold, heavy snows, and a lack of fresh food took a terrible toll. By spring, nearly half of the *Mayflower's* 102 passengers had died.

"…in two or three months' time half of their company died, especially in January and February…"

—*William Bradford,* Of Plymouth Plantation

December 21, 1620
The Pilgrims arrive at Plymouth.

Fall and winter 1620–1621
Illness claims more than 50 lives.

Meeting the natives

At times only six or seven **colonists** were well enough to gather wood, build fires, prepare food, and tend the sick. William Bradford later credited William Brewster and Myles Standish with doing much of the work needed to care for the ill.

On March 16, 1621, the remaining colonists gathered at the meetinghouse. As they were meeting, a tall Wampanoag warrior, armed with bow and arrow, entered the room. He spoke in broken English and told them that his name was Samoset.

A few days later, Samoset returned with Squanto. He told the Pilgrims that the chief of the Wampanoag people was a man named Massasoit. When Massasoit arrived with 60 warriors, the few healthy men at Plymouth reached for their rifles, thinking they might be in danger. What a relief it was to discover that Massasoit had come to offer assistance.

"He [Samoset] told them also of another Indian whose name was Squanto, a native of this place, who had been in England and could speak better English than himself."

—*William Bradford,*
Of Plymouth Plantation

March 6, 1621
Samoset enters Plymouth.

March 22, 1621
John Carver signs a treaty with Massasoit.

The peace treaty

With Squanto as translator, Massasoit and Governor John Carver reached an agreement and signed a **treaty**. Massasoit promised not to harm the Pilgrims. The Pilgrims agreed to aid the Wampanoag if an enemy attacked them. European diseases had killed thousands of American Indians, and warring tribes were threatening the weakened Wampanoag. The agreement helped both the Wampanoag and the Pilgrims. They honored it for the next 40 years.

Samoset greeted the Pilgrims with a few English words that he had learned from British fishermen.

Squanto's gift

Squanto taught the Pilgrims how to plant corn and how to fish. Spring brought better health to most colonists, but it was during this time that Governor Carver died. William Bradford was elected the new governor.

On May 12, 1621, Edward Winslow, whose first wife had died during the winter, married Susanna White, mother of Peregrine (see page 20). Her first husband had also died. This was the first wedding in Plymouth. Governor Bradford performed the ceremony. The Pilgrims considered marriage a legal agreement, not a religious ceremony.

Squanto (about 1600–1623)

In 1614 Squanto was kidnapped from Massachusetts by English explorer Thomas Hunt. He was taken to Spain and sold into slavery. Spanish monks helped him escape and return to North America with another explorer. In 1620 Squanto gave the Pilgrims lifesaving help and guidance. He died in 1623 of fever while on a journey with William Bradford to buy corn from Cape Cod natives.

April 1621
John Carver dies.
William Bradford is elected governor of Plymouth.

April 5, 1621
The *Mayflower* leaves Plymouth to return to England.

Church and state

The Pilgrims did not believe that the government should control the church or that the church should control the government. William Bradford was the political leader. William Brewster was the religious leader. Church (religion) and state (the government) remained separate.

In state or government matters, Myles Standish and Edward Winslow took major roles. Standish's job was to defend or protect the colony. Edward Winslow played a key role in making agreements with the Wampanoag and with the Virginia Company.

This woman, dressed as a Pilgrim, is planting a garden at the re-created Plimoth Plantation.

May 12, 1621
Edward Winslow marries Susanna White. It is the first marriage in Plymouth.

Harvest festival

By fall of 1621, only 53 Pilgrims had survived. They included four married women, five teenage girls, nine teenage boys, thirteen young children, and twenty-two men. Their corn crop did well. They were learning about local plants, fish, and **game**. In October, Governor Bradford decided to hold a celebration. In England, people ate, visited, and played games during harvest festivals.

Massasoit and other American Indians joined the Pilgrims for a harvest festival.

June 1621
The Virginia Company provides a new patent granting the Pilgrims rights to Plymouth and the surrounding land. The Mayflower Compact is no longer needed.

Invited guests

There are two written accounts of this harvest festival that became known as the first Thanksgiving. One is in William Bradford's history, *Of Plymouth Plantation*. The other, written by Edward Winslow, is found in *Mourt's Relation*. According to Winslow, Massasoit and his 90 men stayed in Plymouth for three days.

The Pilgrims served duck and goose. Massasoit and his men contributed five deer. The feast also included fish, eels, lobster, and succotash, a dish made of stewed chicken, beans, and corn. Every family made beer, a common drink at the time. The entertainment included target shooting, games, and contests.

"Our harvest being gotten in, our governor sent four men on fowling [hunting], that so we might after a special manner rejoice together… many of the Indians coming among us, and among the rest their greatest king Massasoit, with some ninety men, whom for three days we entertained and feasted…"

—*Mourt's Relation*

Know It!

In 1863 President Abraham Lincoln made the last Thursday in November a national day of Thanksgiving.

October 1621
What becomes known as the first Thanksgiving is held in Plymouth.

Growing and Changing

In November 1621, another ship, the *Fortune*, arrived with 35 passengers. The **Pilgrims** greeted them warmly. Governor Bradford was stunned to discover that the Virginia Company had not sent any supplies on the *Fortune*. The new settlers did not even have blankets, warm clothing, or any extra food. The **colony** had barely enough food to last the winter. Luckily, clams and shellfish were plentiful. Even so, it was another hard winter.

Plymouth was built on a hillside leading to the sea. The meetinghouse was located at the top of the hill.

Letters home

Various fishing boats and other ships stopped in Plymouth. They often brought letters from England and carried the Pilgrim letters back. Some, like the *Fortune*, brought new **colonists**.

Visitors wrote accounts of life in Plymouth, and so did some of the Pilgrims. Several of these letters and accounts were printed in *Mourt's Relation* in 1622. In 1624 Edward Winslow published another book, *Good News from New England*, which continued the account of life in New Plymouth. The colonists hoped that these accounts would encourage others to join them.

November 1621
The *Fortune* arrives with 35 passengers.

1622
Mourt's Relation is published in England.

A new colony forms

In 1630, 1,000 new settlers reached Massachusetts. These settlers, who were **Puritans**, came in 11 ships loaded with hundreds of cows, horses, pigs, and chickens. They established Massachusetts Bay Colony at present-day Boston (see the map).

Unlike the colonists at Plymouth, the Puritans had money, supplies, and enough workers. Within a few months, 300 to 400 families had established the villages of Charlestown, Watertown, Boston, Roxbury, and Dorchester.

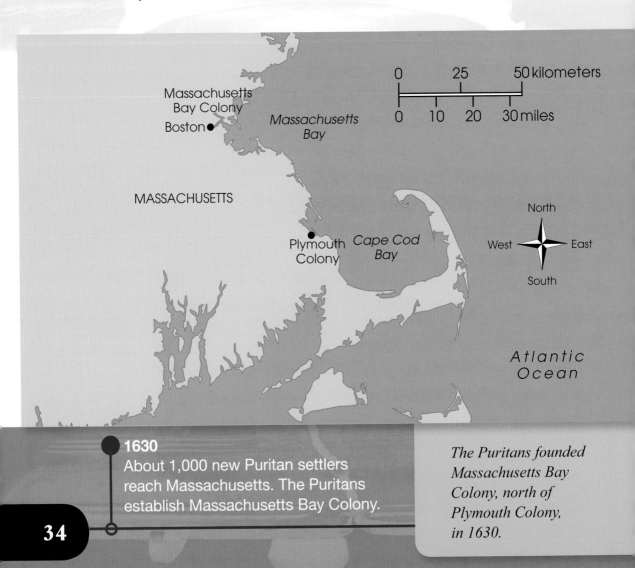

1630
About 1,000 new Puritan settlers reach Massachusetts. The Puritans establish Massachusetts Bay Colony.

The Puritans founded Massachusetts Bay Colony, north of Plymouth Colony, in 1630.

Growth causes problems

Massachusetts Bay and Plymouth colonies often worked together, especially in times of trouble. When the colonies expanded and settlers moved inland, disputes developed with American Indians. In 1637 the colonists fought the Pequot Wars. From 1675 to 1676, they fought Massasoit's son Metacom, who was also called King Philip, in a series of battles called King Philip's War. The peace that had been so carefully established between Massasoit and the original settlers had ended.

Between 1695 and 1765, Massachusetts added 111 new communities. Shipbuilding, shipping, and fishing became major industries. Plymouth remained a small town, but Boston became one of North America's largest cities. By 1775, 15,520 people lived in Boston.

These modern-day men are wearing typical Pilgrim clothing. Plymouth colonists wore bright colors.

1637
The Massachusetts colonists fight the Pequot Wars against American Indians.

1675–1676
The Massachusetts colonists fight King Philip's War against American Indians.

The Mayflower **Compact** first appeared in *Mourt's Relation*, published in 1622. Historians believe that Edward Winslow wrote most of *Mourt's Relation*, and that William Bradford helped him.

Bradford's history

Historians believe that British soldiers may have taken Bradford's history from the Old South Church during the Revolutionary War (1775–1783).

As we have seen, William Bradford, who became governor of Plymouth **Colony**, wrote his own account of the settlement of Plymouth. It was called *Of Plymouth Plantation: 1620–1647*. It contained a copy of the Mayflower Compact. Bradford didn't publish this book, but gave it to his son, who passed it along to his own son. Others borrowed the book. In 1776 it was stored at the Old South Church in Boston. And then it disappeared.

1650
Bradford finishes his book, *Of Plymouth Plantation.*

1776
The colonies declare independence.

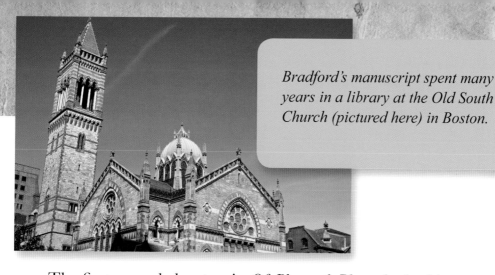

Bradford's manuscript spent many years in a library at the Old South Church (pictured here) in Boston.

The first several chapters in *Of Plymouth Plantation* had been copied by hand into the Plymouth church records. Those records were published in 1841. Where was the rest? In 1855 a U.S. businessman discovered additional parts of Bradford's history in a book published in England. He traced Bradford's original copy to a library there. This important **primary source** of U.S. history was not returned to the United States until 1897.

Available for all

At last, the entire book could be published. Today, everyone can read it and learn about the early days in Plymouth Colony. The copy of the Mayflower Compact in Bradford's book is exactly like the one in *Mourt's Relation*. These two primary source documents—*Of Plymouth Plantation* and *Mourt's Relation*—provide eyewitness accounts of life in New Plymouth.

1855
Of Plymouth Plantation is discovered in England.

1897
Of Plymouth Plantation is returned to Massachusetts.

Preserving *Mayflower* documents

Today, the original version of William Bradford's history, *Of Plymouth Plantation*, is stored at the Massachusetts State Library in Boston. A special **vault** protects it from damage. The vault was designed to control the temperature and humidity (moisture in the air). It also protects the book from fire. The vault was opened in 1961. *Of Plymouth Plantation* was the very first document to be placed inside it.

Of course, Bradford's book was not simply dropped into the vault. First, it was put into a special kind of box for added protection. Light, humidity, and high temperatures can damage books and other paper documents. Bradford wrote his history by hand. The paper and ink are still in good condition, but the cover is not. It is made of vellum, or calfskin. Today, the cover is fragile and can be damaged easily.

Know It!

Even though the original book is not on display, many libraries have a copy of Bradford's *Of Plymouth Plantation*. In addition to being in Bradford's book, the Mayflower Compact is also available on various websites (see page 47).

Can anyone see the book?

Bradford's book is too fragile to go on public display. Librarians only remove it from the vault a few times a year for very special visitors. The librarians always wear clean, white cotton gloves when they handle this valuable document.

The Massachusetts State Library is located in the Massachusetts State House in Boston.

Preserving important documents

State libraries preserve important historical documents. The Massachusetts State Library contains many valuable documents. These include collections of maps, pamphlets, letters, photographs, newspapers, and other items related to the history of Massachusetts and the nation.

Historians use the collection to learn about the state's and nation's history. People studying the history of towns or cities in Massachusetts or doing research into their own family history and property may find useful information in special library collections like the one at the Massachusetts State House.

Know It!

According to the American Library Association, there are more than 122,000 libraries in the United States. Between 2010 and 2011, the Massachusetts State Library was one of 1,113 libraries run by the government. All of these libraries contain primary source documents.

Meet a special collections librarian

"I love to help researchers find the material they need," Elizabeth Carroll-Horrocks says. As a special collections librarian at the Massachusetts State Library, she helps researchers. Some people visit in person. Others call or write the library for information. For example, if someone needs information about Bradford's manuscript, she can help.

Carroll-Horrocks has been working as a librarian in special collections libraries for more than 35 years. To become a special collections librarian, she attended college and then went on to take special classes and earn **degrees** in library science and history. "I love coming to work every day in this historic building," she says. "I enjoy working with great colleagues [coworkers] and the researchers who use the library. Best of all, I like organizing material so that people can find it and use it."

This conservator works to preserve a document.

Plymouth today

Today, Plymouth, Massachusetts, is a modern city. It looks like many other New England towns. None of the original **Pilgrim** homes remain. However, in 1947, a businessman named Henry Hornblower II decided to create a **living history museum** as a way to share his fascination with the Pilgrim story with others. First, he built two Pilgrim-style cottages near the waterfront in Plymouth.

Eventually, Hornblower purchased land in south Plymouth and re-created an entire village. Today, Plimoth Plantation includes 12 Pilgrim homes, a meetinghouse, gardens, and barns. The re-created village is about one-third the size of the original town of New Plymouth. Visitors can watch as actors dressed like Pilgrims do gardening, cooking, and other work. The actors answer visitors' questions about life in the colony.

Plimoth Plantation also includes a Wampanoag village. Here, Wampanoag people demonstrate how their **ancestors** cooked, cured leather, and built **wigwams**.

1947
Henry Hornblower plans a living history museum at Plymouth.

1957
The *Mayflower II* arrives in Plymouth.

The *Mayflower II*

The *Mayflower II* is anchored in Plymouth Harbor. Visitors can climb aboard and visit with actors posing as captain and crew. Builders used primary source documents—like Bradford's history—to create the **replica**.

This model, or replica, of the Mayflower *is called the* Mayflower II. *It was built in England and crossed the Atlantic Ocean to Plymouth, Massachusetts, in 1957.*

Today
About 350,000 people visit Plimoth Plantation each year.

Timeline

1603
James I becomes king of England.

1607
Scrooby Separatists are arrested trying to leave England.

Spring 1608
Separatists begin to successfully leave for Holland.

1609
The Scrooby congregation settles in Leiden.

December 21, 1620
The Pilgrims arrive at Plymouth.

November 21, 1620
The Pilgrims sign the Mayflower Compact.

November 11, 1620
The *Mayflower* reaches Cape Cod. The Mayflower Compact is drafted and signed by passengers. John Carver is elected governor of Plymouth.

Fall and winter 1620–1621
Illness claims over 50 lives.

March 6, 1621
Samoset enters Plymouth.

March 22, 1621
John Carver signs a treaty with Massasoit.

1637
The Massachusetts colonists fight the Pequot Wars against American Indians.

1630
About 1,000 new Puritan settlers reach Massachusetts. The Puritans establish Massachusetts Bay Colony.

1622
Mourt's Relation is published in England.

1650
Bradford finishes his book, *Of Plymouth Plantation*.

1675–1676
The Massachusetts colonists fight King Philip's War against American Indians.

1776
The colonies declare independence.

1855
Of Plymouth Plantation is discovered in England.

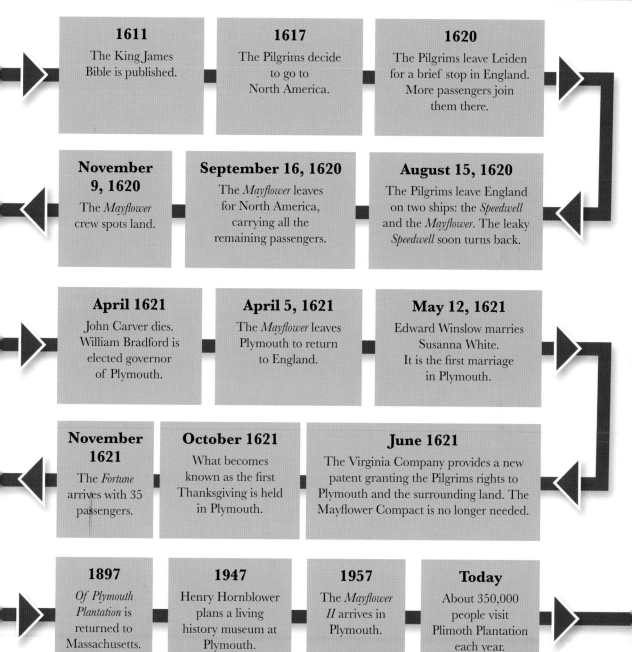

1611
The King James Bible is published.

1617
The Pilgrims decide to go to North America.

1620
The Pilgrims leave Leiden for a brief stop in England. More passengers join them there.

November 9, 1620
The *Mayflower* crew spots land.

September 16, 1620
The *Mayflower* leaves for North America, carrying all the remaining passengers.

August 15, 1620
The Pilgrims leave England on two ships: the *Speedwell* and the *Mayflower*. The leaky *Speedwell* soon turns back.

April 1621
John Carver dies. William Bradford is elected governor of Plymouth.

April 5, 1621
The *Mayflower* leaves Plymouth to return to England.

May 12, 1621
Edward Winslow marries Susanna White. It is the first marriage in Plymouth.

November 1621
The *Fortune* arrives with 35 passengers.

October 1621
What becomes known as the first Thanksgiving is held in Plymouth.

June 1621
The Virginia Company provides a new patent granting the Pilgrims rights to Plymouth and the surrounding land. The Mayflower Compact is no longer needed.

1897
Of Plymouth Plantation is returned to Massachusetts.

1947
Henry Hornblower plans a living history museum at Plymouth.

1957
The *Mayflower II* arrives in Plymouth.

Today
About 350,000 people visit Plimoth Plantation each year.

Glossary

ancestor relative who lived at an earlier time

artifact object created and used by someone in the past

charter legal document granting certain rights and privileges; patent

Christian person who follows the Christian faith

Church of England national church of England

colonial having to do with a colony

colonist person who lives in a colony

colony any people or territory separated from a ruling power

combination agreement that combines two groups of people

compact agreement or understanding between groups of people

congregation group of people gathered for worship, prayer, or other religious event

degree academic award given by a university or college on successful completion of a course of study

Dutch person from the Netherlands, including Holland

game wild animals, including birds and fish, hunted for sport, food, or profit

living history museum museum that tries to re-create a past place or time

patent legal document granting certain rights and privileges; charter

pilgrim traveler or wanderer, especially in a foreign land. When capitalized, it often refers to colonists who settled at Plymouth, Massachusetts, in 1620.

primary source original copy of a journal, letter, newspaper, document, or image

Puritan member of a Christian group who wanted to change the Church of England

recruit to find people for a particular activity, job, or service

replica exact copy

secondary source written account of an event by someone who studied a primary source or sources

Separatist member of a Christian group that wanted to separate from the Church of England

treaty formal agreement between two or more states or groups of people about peace, partnership, trade, or other international relations

vault underground room or chamber

weaver person who makes cloth

wigwam round American Indian home covered with tree bark

Find Out More

Books

Englar, Mary, and Peter McDonnell. *The Pilgrims and the First Thanksgiving*. Mankato, Minn.: Capstone, 2007.

Fradin, Dennis B. *The Mayflower Compact*. New York: Benchmark, 2007.

Harness, Cheryl. *The Adventurous Life of Myles Standish and the Amazing-But-True Survival Story of the Plymouth Colony*. Washington, D.C.: National Geographic Society, 2008.

Waxman, Laura Hamilton. *Why Did the Pilgrims Come to the New World?: And Other Questions About the Plymouth Colony*. Minneapolis, Minn.: Lerner, 2011.

Websites

The Pilgrim Society
www.pilgrimhall.org
Visit Pilgrim Hall to see items that belonged to the Pilgrims.

Plimoth Plantation
www.plimoth.org
To learn more about the Plymouth colony, visit Plimoth Plantation, a living history museum.

Plimoth Plantation: Thanksgiving Interactive
www.plimoth.org/learn/MRL/interact/thanksgiving-interactive-you-are-historian
Investigate the first Thanksgiving at this website.

Secretary of the Commonwealth's Kids' Zone
www.sec.state.ma.us/cis/ciskid/kididx.htm
Visit the Kids' Zone sponsored by the state of Massachusetts.

Yale Law School
http://avalon.law.yale.edu/17th_century/mayflower.asp
See a copy of the Compact and the list of signers.

Index